THIS IS
IMPORTANCE

Other Books by Gregory Betts
Avant-Garde Canadian Literature: The Early Manifestations
The Obvious Flap (with Gary Barwin)
Psychic Geographies and Other Topics
The Others Raisd in Me
Haikube
If Language

THIS IS IMPORTANCE

A Students' Guide to Literature

GREGORY BETTS

Cover image: Rachel Rosen
Cover design: Rachel Rosen
Editor's photograph: Ralph Kolewe
Typeset in Goudy Old Style
Printed by Coach House Printing Company Toronto, Canada

The publisher gratefully acknowledges the support of the Canada Council for the Arts, the Ontario Arts Council and the Canada Book Fund.

Published in Canada by Poplar Press, a division of Wolsak and Wynn Publishers Ltd., Hamilton.

Poplar Press
280 James Street North
Hamilton, ON
Canada L8R 2L3

Library and Archives Canada Cataloguing in Publication

Betts, Gregory, 1975-
   This is importance : a students' guide to literature / Gregory Betts.

ISBN 978-1-894987-75-2

   1. English literature–Study and teaching–Humor. 2. English literature–History and criticism–Humor. I. Title.

PR35.B48 2013   820'.7   C2013-901096-3

This book is dedicated to all those committed to the risk of learning.

CONTENTS

MAKE NO MISTAKE,
MAKE MISTAKES

People make mistakes. We need to in order to learn. When I was a student, I made the mistake of romanticizing nature. I spent my undergraduate summers tree planting in northern British Columbia in the Rocky Mountains. On occasion, I caught glimpses of the sublime nature I had imagined from my readings. I carried a copy of Shelley's poems around with me, and while my co-workers worked, I sometimes skipped off into the forests and glaciers, chanting to all who would listen lines such as:

> The giant brood of pines around thee clinging,
> Children of elder time, in whose devotion
> The chainless winds still come and ever came
> To drink their odours, and their mighty swinging
> To hear, – an old and solemn harmony.

I remember waking early one morning, while everybody else still slept, into such a solemn harmony. My body was still numb from the hard labour of the day before. The closest tents were out of sight and hidden behind giant trees and the folds of a mountain. It was cool and sunny and already light. My tent was pitched in the low arms of an old-growth spruce laced in moss just an arm's length away from a glacial river. My tent, protected by the moss above, had all its sides rolled down into four walls of screen so I had a complete vista. Shelley again: "Power dwells apart in its tranquility, / remote, serene, and inaccessible." And here I was transfixed in its midst.

People, however, aren't the only ones who make mistakes. Across the river, in that thin morning light, I watched an enormous bull moose walking quietly, calmly along the water's edge. It walked in the presumption of its majesty, but it hit a soft patch of earth, snagged, stumbled and came tumbling down, crashing over itself, spilling sloppily, awkwardly into the frigid water. The moose pulled itself up and without even taking the time to shake off, darted directly into the forest – deeply embarrassed. So much for perfect harmony.

In fact, people make a mistake when they say that to err is human. To err is to fall out of harmony with the world – but it is a mistaken, romantic idea to think that such a harmony is true to life or limited to just humans. The Roman philosopher-poet Lucretius, who immortalized in verse the world's first atomic theory, was also the first to write of the absolute importance of error. He believed that if all things worked perfectly inside a harmonious system change would be impossible, that life itself would die. Lucretius developed the idea of the *clinamen* to describe the deviance that occurs inside atoms, within the building blocks of the world. He correctly predicted that sometimes even the particles of atoms swerve and break out of their natural orbit. It is this deviation, he argued, that creates the possibility of chance and change; that creates the very possibility of free will and growth.

Mistakes open up this vista for us. You cannot change unless you break out of what you already know, killing off that which you were before. But like the moose beside the river, change can be awkward and clumsy, and sometimes feel embarrassing. (I won't say that the moose was learning or growing in the human sense, but it certainly was confronting a lack of harmony with its environment.) As writers, as thinkers, as a species, we have made many mistakes, especially about nature and its own will to survive and about the consciousness of other creatures. We make mistaken assumptions about the world, and when the world contradicts our beliefs, we have the opportunity to grow beyond our old understanding of the world. Too often, we dismiss the past because we feel embarrassed about the mistakes made in the process of learning, but progress is nothing more than a great big pyramid built atop a heaped pile of mistakes.

This book is a heaped pile of mistakes! A small pyramid of its own, this book of student mistakes is, then, a document attesting to the personal growth of the thousands of students I have had the wonderful opportunity to teach. One thing that Lucretius missed in his theory of the importance of the error, though, despite all of his genius, was the importance of humour in the process. In my classes, I often start by telling the students that they might come to their education with the faith that they are transforming themselves, which requires killing off part of who they were before. Such intimate change is painful, awkward and often clumsy, and I am there to help them discover their new selves with some measure of – if not grace – then support. Of course, all the while they are learning and unlearning themselves, I am learning and unlearning myself alongside them. So, I am also there to help them see the humour in the process. We do laugh a lot in class: sometimes at my mistakes (for, as all opposites attract too many cooks with rough diamonds in the bush, I take too much pleasure in mixing metaphors and twisting aphorisms, and often get carried away), sometimes at their mistakes (though never singled out as such; humiliation is simply not the point of the game). I have come to learn that laughter and a good sense of humour are essential tools in learning. You fall, you laugh it off and you try again. And then when the video appears on Youtube, you laugh at the slapstick spectacle and grow more resolved to get it right. You can't laugh if you don't see what you did wrong; and you can't really see what you did wrong unless you can laugh at the difference.

The British-Canadian painter and writer Wyndham Lewis says that the basis of humour boils down to two things: things behaving like people, or else people behaving like things. You can picture Charlie Chaplin becoming the assembly-line machine, or else the robot C-3PO (or Commander Data, etc.) behaving almost human. Transgression is funny. (And fun.) In the case of classroom humour, this boundary crossing is subtler: most often, people using the wrong tool inadvertently. In my field, we study tools like literary vocabulary or theoretical concepts and then try to apply them to the interpretation of texts. As the Dadaists and Surrealists discovered a long time ago, if you use the wrong tool, or the right tool in the wrong way, strange and bizarre images emerge. Indeed, you can think of the avant-garde fur-lined teacups or melting clocks as functional precedents for the strange and bizarre images in this book. The more they transgress, the more fun and funnier they are. In fact, André Breton, the founder and leader of the Surrealists, coined the term "black humour" as a way to describe the liberating pleasure of "the superior revolt of the mind." Something wonderful can emerge when you let mistakes happen.

I started writing these mistakes down, building this little but extraordinary pyramid of untruths, as evidence of the learning process, as evidence of the risks my students were taking, but most importantly of all, as evidence of the strange and bizarre images my students were discovering through their mistakes. All teachers end up marking very similar papers on a limited band of topics hundreds of times over every term. It can be tedious work, but it is much less so when you pause to marvel at the inadvertent humour as captured in this book.

There is another way to think of it, though, which leaves the pleasure of the error aside for the moment and considers the broader connection between human cultures and mistakes. There is an aphorism that claims that people make deities out of what they cannot understand. Conversely, however, we also tend to mock and deride things when we do not yet understand them. When something new and true appears within human culture it must, by necessity, disrupt something old and (now) false. The immediate temptation is to discredit the new insight as an error, a mistake, regardless of how it was discovered or uncovered or merely stumbled upon. You must be mistaken, we say. It couldn't be true, we claim, because that would mean what we currently believe is false: as if that were a plausible defence of anything. But the end result of any new insight being incorporated is the gradual realization that the other way, the old way, was indeed wrong. Were the old ways just mistakes? Not always, certainly – sometimes the new ways are just new mistakes introduced – but perhaps yes, we were wrong before (and this possibility is not to be feared!). I would hasten to add that even the old mistakes were each useful to their moment. And as errant as they might have been, they certainly played a role in correcting other mistakes or else in prompting us to move on.

Science has helped to teach us that human knowledge has been continually undone and remade for thousands of years as we push those deities of the unknown ever further into the recesses of the universe. Let us not stop this process ever! Let all truths be challenged and tested and revised when they falter. I have no doubt that our conception of the world will be undone and redone a thousand times over in the future course of human history. Thinking about the broad sweep of human knowledge from this perspective is to recognize the important role of the mistake inside human culture. Our understanding of the world is temporary, fragile and constantly changing. It moves like a clumsy moose crashing and stumbling through time, only occasionally affording thin moments of grace and solemn harmony. When we learn, when we take the risk of making our own mistakes, we play out in miniature the transformation of human knowledge on the larger scale of time. Crashing and thrashing and stumbling towards constant reinvention and forms of renewal, only thus do we learn. Indeed, mistakes show up especially in our moments of most committed learning.

All of these mistakes open up new possibilities, new chances to discover things we cannot even imagine until they become known. But if all the old ways are mistakes of a sort, and all truths only temporary, then this compendium of student errors becomes, in the end, just a compendium of distortions of distortions. All we know is still subject to chance and change, and change will lead us to change forevermore. It is not a mockery, then, that glimmers in the laughter in this book; it is an opening, or an exit, from the truth for just a moment. Its pleasure, I suspect, dwells in that revolt.

Looking back at Shelley, now, after so many years of teaching, I discover that – my mistake – this was part of his message all along. The majesty of nature was not the result of some fixed harmony, or the discovering of some fixed truth, but of the chance to break out of the limitations of human knowledge if just for a fleeting, ever-turning moment:

And this, the naked countenance of earth,
On which I gaze, even these primeval mountains,
Teach the adverting mind.

IN THE BEGINNING WAS MYTH

Myth is a story that has been passed over by generations of generations. It is a tale that doesn't need to be real to be forgotten.

The universe is unknown, unexplained, even to the reader who remains in an overwhelming state of confusion. Only the author knows everything.

I don't even want to believe myths.

God created himself. Emphasis draws attention.

The only symbol from the Bible that we still know today is the dove that flew away.

The Greek and Roman gods were ineffectual when it came to hair.

Helen of Troy is a historical woman who chose a controversial partner.

The invention of the wheel was the beginning of the revolution.

An example of a myth is the belief that Canada had a beginning.

Myth is the belief that authors can achieve fame, fortune and righteousness in Canada.

Myth is a broken telephone without a dialtone.

Bias writes all literature, but none more than myth and all the works we have studied thus far.

Myth is anything not real.

Literary and Critical Minds

As critics, many writers like to say that others are wrong.

Unless different approaches to thematic criticism are applied, long term deformation in the shape of Canadian literature could result.

When Darwin hit the Earth, he had a great impact.

Atwood makes the assertion that Britain is an island. She then claims that writing is a work of art. Atwood proceeds to discuss her suggestions where she outlines the criticisms to her discussion.

Thematic critics have no use for language.

The brilliance of Albert Einstein never ceases to exist.

Einstein is suggestive of humanity's greatest downfall.

Criticism is a critical method.

Some critics disagree on weather that is good.

It is the struggle that makes people readers.

Every sentence is a subject of the trees.

On Narrative Form

Characters are all born in literary Canada.

Rising Action is the period before the climax where there is a build-up to prepare the reader for the ultimate high.

The narrator is bias.

All literary devices die.

The average reader expects grammar and punctuality in every sentence.

Female protagonists take no heed to spiritual warnings.

The story is so complicated, so devious, that nobody could possibly understand it, let alone me.

It is certain that there is no conclusion.

Writing is one way to control the truth.

An unreliable narrator is one whose recitation of the plot is strongly compromised because of madness, blindness or biasness.

The past tense represents an attempt to reflect on what has already happened to the narrator, such as future failure.

Realist writers have both feet grinding in the world.

Form causes everything.

The author speaks volumes in his novel.

The narrative is the experience of everything: everything that can happen.

A period in a sentence suggests death.

On Poetry

The poem begins with the poet's language.

The poet attempts to salvage that which is beyond recovery.

Poetry has many complex dimensions: it can be revolting or disgusting.

Language makes the poem seem a certain way.

Seeing 4 lines per stanza makes you believe that it is a Quartrain.

Language is extremely useful to a writer.

A narrator is the unreliable voice inside a poem. We find this out at the very end.

On Reading

Reading is a painful experience, although pleasurable.

Reading creates a sinister impression of the imagination.

Readers tend to miss the deeper meaning of a text because they tend to focus on me.

On the Novel

The novel is religion in Canada.

War is the point of the novel.

Japanese-Canada is a novel.

Writers take your history, but give it back to you.

Without the novel, film adaptation would not be so successful.

The book lacks the soundtrack of a film.

A novel does not have a soundtrack.

Audiences are disappointed because novels are too long.

Without sound or images, the film would be lacking. Like a novel.

DEFINITIONS I
Types of Narrators

First Person Narration: the narrator can only see his own point.

Third Person Narration: the narrator gets to know the main characters.

Third Person Narration: is when the narrator doesn't care.

Third Person Narration: the narrator is involved with another plot.

Omniscient Narration: stories told by God.

Limited Narrator: has nothing to say.

Homodiegetic Narrators have issues of sexual orientation in their voice.

The narrator is a vital.

Homodiegetic: the narrator's main focus is to learn something, to teach himself something.

A homodialectic narrator probably knows "the language" of gay homosexuals.

The camera is an objecting narrator.

Hamartia (Tragic Flaw)

Hamartia is tied to Harmony and used in poetry and literature to create canned ideas through words that sound similar.

Hamartia is a sense of compassion, sympathy and sorrow felt by the reader for a courageous character.

Hamartia is the gift of love.

The term hamartia means irony or satire. Like when your professor lectures the class on turning off cell phones and then his phone goes off (;-)).

Very hamartian.

Hamartia is the bleeding of two perspectives into one work.

Hamartia is the teaching of a child in martial contexts. The study of teaching martial arts. A mother teaching her child to behave, survive, speak, make martial art.

Hamartia conveys a sense of unity throughout a literary work, counteracting differences within a text.

Hamartia is a term from Aristotle to discuss the animals in his country.

Hamartia is the ability of an author to discuss things they aren't knowledgeable about.

Hamartia is how the "tragic hero" meets demiss.

Hamartia means to describe a certain object by using a musical song to describe it.

Hamartia is a Christian hero from Greek times.

Symbolism

Symbolism is when an author uses one thing to stand on another.

Symbolism uses language to guide writing beyond reality.

Symbolism describes an indescribable object.

I think symbolism means something else.

Symbolism: the notion that something is a body and meaning is attached to it.

Symbollism is when the author doesn't care to tell the truth.

Symbolism is using an object to force the reader to remember something else like in realism.

Symbols are an attempt to incubate an abstraction.

Symbolism: one more thing in this world that isn't itself.

Realism

Realism takes itself literally.

A text is almost always a memisis of life, but realism is when life stays faithful to its cause.

Realism reflects someones perscription of reality.

Realism happens, whereas only authors believe in symbolism.

Realism is when there is no meaning in a story.

The Sketch Genre

A sketch is a short person with a lot of colourful descriptions.

A sketch is a narrative that makes a small town seem more uninhabitable.

A sketch describes a small plot of land in central Ontario on which the Moodie's lived.

A sketch is a comedy that takes place in Canada.

A sketch is a quick slapshot of life.

A sketch offers real insight into the lives of an autobiography.

A sketch is where the author is. These stories usually have irony in them like Janus.

A sketch has no motives, no plot, nor style.

The sketch genre is one that encourages 19th Century Canadians. Susanna Moodie is a strong example of a sketch genre.

The use of sketches, particularly fictional sketches, is an effective way for the writer to encourage foreigners to come to Canada.

When author's have personal feelings, they are sketching.

Irony

Irony is a transformer with more than meets the eye.

When irony is deployed it kills the sense of the reader.

EUROPEAN ART AND LITERATURE
William Shakespeare

The author, being William Shakespeare, uses I am a Pentameter in his sonnet.

In Shakespeare's poems, he uses people such as nature, beauty and time. He does use people in a more earthly manner.

During the Renaissance, society viewed women as the feminine representation, which, consequently, have their meaning in relationship to men.

Hamlet is confused by the outer world, though he belongs there.

Everybody fails the test on *Hamlet*, even Hamlet.

Alexander Pope

The Genre of "The Rape of the Lock" is a mopic.
The mopic was written in order to end innocent fun.

Belinda. A fair maiden of her time, who unrealistically
does not have to worry about life other than to look
beautiful. One would love to be her shoes.

Satire attempts to deflate a subject, like attire.

Alexander Pope claims to camouflage the walls of
humour.

This begs the question, why would Pope make a
satire intended for humourless people?

Superficial, shallow and clothesminded Belinda.

This was a time when getting up was a big hassle
for men and women.

Jonathan Swift

This author is writing about his fondess of Ireland and his dislike of foreign things such as furniture.

The Romantics

In the Romantic period, there were no social conflicts, hence, the poets were all romantic.

These Romanticist poets are no longer understandable by modern teens.

Samuel Taylor Coleridge

The Mariner has almost become like Jesus because he travels from place to place looking for people who don't want to hear what he has to say.

Jesus and the Ancient Mariner are very similar in this case because they were both singled out from their peers and given something to wear.

Shooting the albatross is worse than Jesus.

Percy Bysshe Shelley

Shelley is, in a sense, an author for he too has a sneering expression.

Mary Shelley's *Frankenstein*

The goal of life, for many, is to discover immorality. Victor Frankenstein desires this gravely.

Later on, Frankenstein gives up the thought of ever finding someone who can look inside of him.

The Ancient Mariner was different from Frankenstein because he wasn't disfigured or brought to life unnaturally.

Mary Shelley's text uses an unrelatable narrator in *Frankenstein*.

The question of Mary Shelley's sanity perspires throughout the entire text.

The book lives in a frame.

Curiosity killed the cat, but no cat ever created a monster.

Lewis Carroll

Neologisms are the beasts of language.

Killing a Jabberwocky is childish. Fact.

Who do your words belong to? Well, Carroll's words belong to no one.

Neologisms help a reader to not understand a poem.

Sigmund Freud

Freud was looking for little girl dreams to undermine.

Freud's abilities to make concise conclusions so efficiently demonstrates his successful narrative farming technique.

He does this by first undermining his unreliability.

Freud attributes psychoneurosis to patients for their responses to his dreams.

All of Freud's dreams seem to be caused by her childhood sexuality.

Freud, being a psychologist, is attempting to explain and prove the hysteria of young women.

The Modernists

Free writing limits language by metaphorically
butchering it. Such a dreary spectacle of language.

Marlow does not understand the Mr. Kurtz way
as he does not appear to have any morals.

The First World War was a genre of poetry that
emerged early in the century.

The poet uses war as a central image of conflict.

André Breton

Breton's poem illustrates that murder is not a
logical means to express anger since it is too
intimate.

If the reader commits a murder, the reader is
therefore directly involved with the murder.

The repetition of the hard 'c' makes murder seem
unappealing to the reader. It requires too much effort.

The speaker causes the reader to rationally realize that being a crowd and murdering someone the same way as Jesus is difficult.

The second stanza of Breton's poem illusions a murder in the mid-evil era. This era is not as intimate as killing Jesus.

The final stanza depicts murder by air. This murder requires being a "psychopath" which is a label most readers would consider unappealing.

In the end, it is probably better to use imagination, instead of actual murder, to release anger.

Samuel Beckett

Krapp's Last Tape has to go to bathroom but can't. The banana is something to hold on to.

Bananas are an old man's life.

Bananas are a temptation few can resist.

Dada and Surrealism

The Dadaists tried hard to be misunderstood. The Surrealists, in contrast, we're interested in the sexy unconscious.

The roll of women in surrealism is rarely covered.

Living irrational is an inevitable way to live.

James Joyce

Portrait of the Artist is the same as everything else Joyce ever wrote. The entire novel is filled with Joyce and women, described as white, described as being chaste.

Sometimes Joyce uses the colour red to represent blood, such as in the scene where Stephen bleeds – it is described as being "red."

When Bonanza closed down, James Joyce left his narrative.

In a Marxist reading of "Araby," we have to wonder about the workplace safety of the workers at the bazaar and whether or not they have health insurance.

"Araby" contains gendered stains and gasps.

Joyce casts doubt into the stream-of-consciousness.

PROFOUND FORISMS I

The author uses a forism to express a commonly held belief.

Atomization is about atoms flowing around in space.

Beauty is temporary therefore one should procreate.

Mortality is the result of time.

The alphabet has been a major influence on many poets.

In general, poets are striving to generate taboos.

When lust presents itself as attainable, desperate bachelors act on the opportunity.

Reality is hard to live in.

School makes men dream of war.

Homeless people are undeniably alive.

Most people do not know that they fear what they do not know.

Sexual orientation hurts parents.

We know nothing of reality.

In conclusion, it is always important to know which work is being read.

Children are a stigma of innocence.

There is never a situation where coherency can exist.

Death can be viewed as a bad position. Perhaps the worst.

Exposition is the future before the flashback.

Literature is a very important mode of transportation.

Marxism theories the text.

I get a shady feeling from story telling.

Most people worry about customized babies.

It is difficult to bomb someone softly.

LITERARY CANADA
Small Town Canada

People in small towns share, exchange and steal goods that they were not able to grow. Whereas in the city, there is no room to bury things.

In the imagination of Canadians (as well as reality) the prairies are an empty place. One prairies is the same as another.

It is clear that already the younger generation is not sure if they wish to dedicate the rest of their lives to moving away to Toronto.

Canadian Cities

The most barbaric thing in Montreal is the construction of steps, which interfere with walking.

It is better to take sufficient time to consider and develop a negative view of Canadian cities.

Prostitutes frown society.

This Canadian city contributes to individual disappointments and continual failure. Therefore, insanity.

Hockey

Terry Sawchuk is so tough he doesn't even know how to spell victemhood.

Hockey came to Canada through an immigrant family.

The best hockey players wear no special outfits. And I'm not talking about nothing.

The gaolie is a very gory position.

Hockey players say, "Look at me" and "Look at how in control I am." This is because, in real life, they only know how to detect where a puck goes.

Hockey ruins faces.

The five-hole IS erotic.

It is acceptable for Canadians to disrespect their
spouses for hockey, because hockey is part of
their identity. Canadians realize that hockey is
mandatory.

Hockey is sexually lewd behaviour.

CANADIAN LITERATURE
The Confederation Era

At the turn of the twentieth century, writers were a minority amongst Canadian writers.

It is marginal to find a voice in Canada.

Technological advances, such as the printing press, had an impact on the books by Bliss Carmen, Archibald Lampmen, Charles Roberts and Duncan Scott.

Both Roberts and Carman are places themselves within the landscape.

Although many authors are fictional, Margaret Atwood says that many carry a "Canadian" tone. The characters suffer for this.

Before Confederation, the First World War took refuge in the Canadian wilderness. The First World War was one of many battles taking place at the time. Nature was Canada's best technology.

We experience the wild, they experienced the wilderness.

Canada is lacking animals because of their depiction in poetry.

Ernest Thompson Seton

Earnest Thompson Seton and Duncan Campbell D. C. Scott are effective in their causes, whether it be the extinction of a human race, or the conservation of animals, they are both committed to natural beauty.

Seton's founding of the Boy Scouts further sparks his quest to investigate young boys in their wilderness.

Lobo, like most protagonists within literature, has a woman named Blanca.

Logos is defeated only when his villain kidnaps logos love.

Susanna Moodie

Moodie loves to beat up Canada.

Moodie describes herself as a woman she comes into contact with. Some would say "frequently."

Moodie's writing read as if they were written by someone with a much less schooling.

She is not the same as other people.

Moodie is uncommon in Canada for not returning to England when she is done with this country.

Moodie gives enough detail to feel right in bed with her best characters. This is because Moodie's aim is convince readers not to go to Canada.

Her food is too spicy for the Bush.

For Moodie, Montreal is a source of cholera.

When Moodie realizes that she is no longer in England, she begins to lose her human perspective. Nature is a broom in this case.

Both of the author's birthplaces influence her.

In the end, Moodie is happy with her heroin.

Anna Jameson

Mrs. Jameson never forgot the look of a hammer.

Jameson needs her readers to have a sense of humour in order to make sense of her.

Anna James finds old characters and is amused. In this sentence, old can be taken to mean not new.

Mrs. Jameson and Susanna Moodie are both profilic writers from the last eighteen centuries.

They do this through a series of sketches that describe a long Canadian winter.

Although Mrs. Jameson realizes the presence of the masses is inevitable, it is still definitely a sore eye for the traveller.

Charles G. D. Roberts

Charles G. D. Roberts fathered Canadian poetry. He found the poems in nature.

He believes that Canada does not yet know how great it will be. The best thing he loves about Canada is its charismatic lack.

Roberts is unique, however, as he is a great number of puns.

The Patriarchal sonnet is the traditional form for the flight of the geese to warmer climates.

Roberts is an unnatural premise, an artistic produce of Canada.

Marjorie Pickthall

Although her story is told, Pickthall confirms that she is dead.

E. Pauline Johnson

Pauline Johnson knows that when men do not conform to opposites they are called effeminate.

Johnson was raised as a young lady but grew out of it.

Her preference for the questionable is very much a native tradition.

Pauline Johnson wrote this poem to surprise me.

Susan Frances Harrison (a.k.a. "Seranus")

Susan Frances Harrison, one of the Canadian song birds, elevates the Falls despite herself. She was one of the founders of "Early Canada."

Harrison runs out of words in describing manmade wonders, such as Niagara Falls.

The British equivalent to the Falls is a pond, a mere pond.

Archibald Lampman

Archibald Lampman is full of horrifying imagery. It represents the fear that humanity will be replaced by inhumanity.

The predominant faith of Europeans at this time was Christianity and this Hell would have surrounded Lampman during his upbringing.

Fear in the mind is a feared phenomenon. Lampman, however, is not a vampire.

A group of Canadian poets, led by Archibald Lampman, were withered down to a dull and stagnant creature by the incessant routine of the city. At that time, all humans were extinct, or so it seemed. The only character was gluttony.

Lampman wrote about his demise in "The City of the End of Things." This is the grim idiocy at the heart of it all.

The city was overpopulated by three people. For if humans build cities, they will become slaves.

Humans in the wilderness are cities.

Lampman's life was an ominous routine, like a monotonous idiot. Only nature could put an end to it. He probably hated Toronto.

Lampman's poetry is as terrifying as Carman's, but his is more rhythmic and evil.

Archibald Lampman fears that the future could happen again.

Duncan Campbell Scott

Like Susanna Moodie, D. C. Scott would like us to give up our dreams for the sake of orphans.

Fiction is his way of faking it.

D. C. Scott has a limited relationship to his characters.

D. C. Scott is a homodiagenetic narrator because he is the story of two houses.

At the height of the land, he is telling the reader about the boring north. He has a moment that only comes once every so often. It is called "Something." This is what he has to give up in order to get home. His guides do not wake up.

Canada has rarely used a first person's narrator.

Scott's writing does not allow readers to ignore the words.

Isabella Valancy Crawford

Isabella Valancy Crawford represents nature to fall in love with. For example in "Love Me, Love My Dog," the page in the poem knows who Lady Clare is based on who likes his Chieftain's dog. "Ho" thought the page, "She loves his hound."

Crawford is the kind of woman who likes men to give her forgive-me-nots.

The dying relationship in "The Hidden Room" will last forever, symbolizing the death they once shared.

ENGENDERED PROFOUNDISMS

Sex is over sexualized.

Visually, the femme fatale on the screen is gorges.

Male power is surreal and rooted in the un-mind.

Females are outside the inside of society. The texts depict women as outsiders on the inside, that women were outsiders within, and this position is questioned in and excluded from society.

The presence of a character's voice denotes that her voice is being used.

In Western societies male members are expected to display masculine traits. Traits such as aggressiveness to heroines.

Women were amusing men to inspire art. The men would often muse the women, especially nude.

She is destroyed at the end of the film and that brings her back into the traditional female role.

The lecture on Tuesday discussed the emergence of minorities such as women. Women are considered 'not existed' outside of the marriage system.

Being educated, one could say they were barely women any more.

When labializing an area the reader is constantly thinking of what they know of that area.

Female writing has no reality.

Her language makes the reader question reality.

Organizing knowledge in any way makes that knowledge patriarchal.

MODERN CANADA
Lucy Maude Montgomery

Anne of Green Gables started off low and it had something to do with her being an orphan. However, with her ambiguous mind, she developed a liberal mindset.

Anne is a scholar. This is a place in society. This is a huge feet for a little orphan girl from nowhere.

Anne needs to have an income or else Marilla will have to sell herself.

Both *Anne* and *Sunshine* use locale as part of their setting.

Montgomery creates pitcheresque scenery that captures her readers and carries them away.

Stephen Leacock

Stephen Leacock is considered to be a humouristic novel.

Leacock's work describes the small town of Maripoza, full of zany inhabituals, like the Pathetic Knights who sink a boat to show their love for Canada.

Sunshine Sketches humorously depicts the stereos of a small town.

Leacock's Mariposa is a city like New York or London only without the people. The streets are very wide.

The Nights of Pithias are a group of drinkers in the Temperance movement. They go out in the evening, on ferries, to 'have a good time.'

The Church burning is funny because we all think like that. You have to laugh at your morality.

The narrator in *Shine Sketches* depicts the monster mass meeting satirically.

Robert W. Service

Robert Service's "Shooting Old Dan and Grew" carries within its violent dirty pages not one redeeming factor.

It is worth noting that the stranger in "The Shooting of Dan McGrew" enters the bar from the outside.

Lou, the woman at the bar, represents the feminine power overcoming the masculine form of sex appeal. Therefore, masculinity is defeated by manliness disguised as femininity in this situation.

Unlike in Grainger's *Woodsmen of the West*, there is no overt masculinity to be found in war. See Robert Service for this. He was a female stretcher bearer.

E. J. Pratt

His poem is disguised as a shark.

John McCrae

McCrae, like the people in his poem, had to be dead in order to write "In Flanders Fields."

Frank Prewett

Frank Prewett's "Card Game" shocks with how somebody could pick up and leave a card game in order to save lives.

Once dead, a soldier is dead. He will not return home. This is the result of ignoring the war.

The poem is a horror of war.

Sinclair Ross

Sinclair Ross does not allow his characters the laughter that would have flourished them.

Mrs. Bentley stays alive as a character because it was not the end of the novel. She remains a solid.

Mrs. Bentley is a typical woman, unlike the Depression.

She is able to stay calm and collected in her matter.

Mrs. Bentley opens a bookstore with Phillip to start a new chapter in her life.

She is an artist because she can see people in the nude light.

Philip trades his lifestyle into a bookstore.

Sinclair Ross' life is very biographical. It is worth noting that his biography influenced his life.

Because the book did not sell very well, it is regarded as Canadian.

Instead of showing empathy, Judith is releaved that Judith dies. This also puts a strain on her relationship with Philip.

Philip does not get intimate with his wife, something expected of priests.

Morley Callaghan

Father Dowling has something he wants to give the prostitutes.

Father Dowling's urge to help Ronnie and Marge stem from his education in the semenary. They are tangible things within his society that he can use to help himself.

Toronto is filled to the brimstone with pagans.

He wants to erase the girls with their sins.

He has a heart on for the girls ☺.

Callaghan does not use the elements to solve the conflict in his novel.

Callaghan's literature deals quasi-specifically with Toronto.

From a symbolic view the book does not contain a lot of symbolism; however Callaghan's writing is overtly symbolic. His thoughtful mind always shines.

Callaghan uses prostitution to show that his novels take place in Toronto.

CONTEMPORARY CANADA

There was a literal explosion in Canadian Literature after 1950.

Patrick Lane describes four different things that Canadian literature falls on.

Robert Kroetsch uses imagery because he is a poet in love with a painter.

Margaret Atwood

Canadian tales are always traumatic experiences. See, for instance, Margaret Atwood.

I tried to use the Post Structure to build my argument about Margaret Atwood.

Atwood is typical of the narrator who knows little and experiences even less. Her characters are confused about their point.

The poetry of Margaret Atwood and Alfred Purdy share the same similarities.

Both Atwood and Purdy frequently use death as a symbol of the inability to survive.

Margaret Atwood's theory of survival barely applies to her own writing.

Atwood's protagonists often lack the female body.

Margaret Atwood used settings in, not just her poems, but her novels as well.

Margaret Atwood uses mages of nature throughout her poetry.

As a foreigner, Margaret Atwood does not understand Canada.

Atwood gives freedom to her readers by confusing them. In fact, the narrator does this work for her.

Atwood is able to get across the stereotypes that come with being Canadian, such as Rednecks. By writing this, she is able to express our nation to others who may not believe her.

Offred throws up herself into the hands of the resistance.

Offred enters the flashback scene from the future. There she discovers what she already knew.

Offred is some kind of sexy, but not the pleasing kind. She is more like a narrative function.

She lives in a place that restricts women's right to speak for a long time. Therefore, she communicates through the male gaze.

Kat, in "Hairball," has an identity that lives in the sphere of consumer culture. She had it surgically removed.

Atwood bares her victimization, but Munro survives the experience.

Canadians are victimized by having to fight Margaret Atwood for survival.

Canadians paint the theme "survival" onto their books.

Sheila Watson

The narrative style is omnimpotent.

James can not see that he is not viewed as very respectable.

He, like a child, has adultery with Angel.

As a result, the text is not being looked at as literature, but a piece of work.

It is questionable whether the novel has taken place.

Mordecai Richler

Barney detaches himself from his wife by his death. This is something he will come to reject.

After reading the book, we do not necessarily understand the ending.

Alzheimers is perfect for Canadians.

The Clara Charnofsky Foundation celebrates female artists with her name.

The adaptation remains faithful to the theme of adultery.

Dionne Brand

As an experimental writer, she inevitably has drawbacks.

In *What We Along For*, Tuyen is an Avon Guard artist who doesn't want to serve her family.

Books set in Toronto are automatically not realistic.

The Small Press

What makes the Small Press unique is that they use no criteria to publish a work.

This is what makes the Small Press addictive.

TISH is the manifestation of otherwise unpublishable work.

Filling Station hosted numerous events which lasted for two years.

Some Canadian poets embraced this ideal and Louis Cabri as well.

Andrea Jarmai uses a lot of high fluting words.

Al Purdy

Al Purdy writes about places in Canada that are unable to be uninhabited.

Nobody expects Al to be beautiful.

Margaret Atwood loves Al Purdy.

Al Purdy displays the dangers of the Western Canadian Lifestyle. However, in "The Country North of Belleville," the author shifts his focus to the disappearance of eastern Ontario.

Purdy is also engaged to the landscape.

Nicole Brossard

Brossard has a hard time interpreting her own book.

"Lorna's naked body" provides an image into the idea of the female body that needs to be reread to be believed.

Women are killed at the end of novels.

It is entirely possible that the book was consciously constructed, and that Brossard's decisions are deliberate.

Daphne Marlatt

Marlatt, in using Cixous, reconstructs herself into an organism of equal representation for women.

Daphne Marlatt represents language as being in stable.

George Elliott Clarke

George Elliott Clarke shows how Africadians suffer from the Blues and the Bible.

George Elliott Clarke is an excellent writer who expresses himself through his heritage ties.

Clarke proves that coloured people experience the world in black and white.

George Elliott Clarke and E. J. Pratt are considered to be revolting to Eastern Canada.

Clarke is an Afraidian author.

According to Clarke, if the morbid is one cool of literature, the erotic is the other.

Margaret Laurence

The Stone Angle is a song about a statue in Manitoba.

There is no excuse for a man not to try and find himself a good wife.

Hagar tried to pass ideology to her son John by playing store with him.

Therefore, Mr. Currie is a man who values his hardship.

He believes he is of a higher class than other citizens and thinks no man can make a decision for himself, hence, he is considered a liberal.

She also shares beliefs of the Liberal political ideologist, such as education, and hard work in climbing the economic ladder.

In Hagar's situation, she used her right and opportunity to marry Bram Shipley who later became her husband.

Be it his family, his community, or nature itself; they all wore his adornments. His children were trophies.

bpNichol

bpNichol loves to touch people. Sometimes he does this by reading inside their minds.

bpNichol believed that language stemmed from the alphabet.

bpNichol broke the boundaries. He remains opposite to contrary.

bpNichol is known for the Assassination of a Horseman.

Sound poetry as a whole expands the written form to a more sensory level, especially the olfactory element.

bpNichol shows that nature is beautiful by comparing it to death.

bill bissett

bill bissett does not belong in what Karasick
refers to as the "real world" (63).

bill bissett's work is to put it plainly linguistic sex.

bissett feels like a whale in a forest, at least that's
what his readers think.

Michael Ondaatje

The English Patience only has one book, called
Herodotus, which is the Greek god of history of
the desert.

By colonizing the landscape of her body, Almasy
encroaches on her nation.

History is the portions of life recorded here and
there, time to time.

Christian Bök

Constraint-based poetry is poetry with orthographic restrictions. For instance, when a poem lacks a certain alphabet.

Christian Box's poetry does not go so far as to make sense.

Bök's writing is devoid of any sort of humanity or human connection.

Eunoia is a text that limits its chapters to the use of only one towel each.

Helen of Troy used to date free verse poets, but is now physically constrained. Free verse has no chance with meaning. The battle between Greeks and the Trojans was basically like the contemporary poets and free verse. Helen, on the other hand, is saved by math.

Christian Bök is a pun.

Sound Poetry

Sound poetry requires a certain mindset to fully comprehend and I do not have it, yet.

Sound poetry should not man but be.

Timothy Findley

In his book, *THE WARS*, the author Timothy Findley waits until the war is done to tell his story. We call this a retrospective look at WW II values.

The reader is comfortable with Findley and takes a relaxing stroll through his relationship with Nature.

He portrays nature as a harmonious relationship among animals.

For example, in *The Wars* by Timothy Finally, we witness Robert Ross' ideology quit a lot.

During the course of this novel the descriptions of animals are read from the beginning to the end.

Living through war is a violent experience. You have to sneak around.

War is not necessarily a good activity because just like those animals that end up dead, humans also do lose their lives. However during certain occasions it becomes necessary for us to wage wars against each other in order to have peace. It will get even worse.

Dennis Lee

In his essay on "Cadence, Country, Silence: Writing in a Colonial Space," Dennis Lee is primarily concerned with what it means to be a Canadian flag.

Lee invented the idea of silence. He was one of the first to stop talking in Canada in the 1960s. Lee is interested in the fact of Canada's status as a colon.

For Lee, poetry is a flower that fertilizes itself.

Leonard Cohen

Leonard Cohen's poem use personification in attributing human qualities to a manimate object. He also uses frequently the technique of "in jamming."

He compares the kite to a fish, which gives it human characteristics.

Cohen sits at a bar, revealing personal things about himself, until the reader comes along to connect to his realness.

When Cohen goes to the beach, it feels warm.

Reading Niche transformed him into a punchy, lewd poetise. There is still a romantic notion that music may be seen in his poetry.

Being Jewish, Cohen spoke out against the oppression in his poetry.

Leonard Cohen might not be a typical winter, due to his success as a singer and songer.

Alice Munro

Lives of Girls and Women falls under the genre of Southern Ontario. This is actually a subcategory of the main genre called Real. This genre usually address the ugly cures for life.

Munro's text *Live Girls and Women* is about coming in sex and femalehood.

Everything in society is unacceptable, especially the sexy.

Although, today's society is more conversational about sex, alcohol, drugs, and so on, the reality is that everybody just lies just the same.

When the text is as ambiguous as its author, we have to assume that we are reading Alice Munro and not one of her characters.

Throughout her writing there is strong evidence that Munro has feelings of her own.

Fern is also described as contour shape, which suggests that the shape of her body is being sexy.

She is prohibited to express herself because it threatens society; something that is only done by males.

She wears a too-true-to-life disguise.

Munro seems to be aware of her characters.

Fiona's inability to remember inhibits her memory.

Thomas King

In comparison with Atwood, Thomas King is a short story.

He is not an ideal Canadian or American, therefore he must be Blackfoot.

Gail Scott

Gail Scott has created a new style of prose writing that is literally not read.

The Farm Show

The idea was to take a group of actors out of their natural habitat and show them to farmers.

A play without a story line or plot is a huge success.

The play does not follow traditional stanzas.

The actors wanted to capture the fibre of the folk.

Parents make successful farmers.

If you can't make ends meet on your farm, you need to get dinosaurs or giant apples. Others make a living by leaving. Lee Jarvis has a "duck-pond" with deer.

The Farm Show was an international success in Clinton, Ontario.

Frank Davey

Frank Davey argues against the fallacy of literature.

Davey is a detriment to Canadian Literature.

Davey's essay is about the problems of reducing a text to a paraphrase, and why critics should never do it.

Thematic criticism also prefers the mundane Davey.

Michael Turner

Joe Dick is the epiphany of a typical anti-conformist.

Joe and Billy like to experience each other's dialogue. The book, however, refuses to show them talking.

Joy Kogawa

When reading Joy Kogawa's *Obasan*, I was impressed with the way that the author levitated the Japanese Canadians to dignified levels.

Joy Kogawa provides a recount of Japanese Canadian experiences.

The primary task is that Obasan has to master the language of silence and the language of speech. She grows more and more attentive to silent language.

There is often violence of the hen towards the young chicks and violence of people towards chickens.

It is true, however, that Kogawa's letters contain letters.

In the novel *Obasan* by Joy Kogawa, silence plays a big party in the storyline.

Kogawa's cadence had been in her life for a long time because the thoughts she wrote about had been there before she wrote them.

Bryan Lee O'Malley

The satireness put a CBC logo on Scott Pilgrim's shirt.

Scott is weird, odd, possibly enjoys watching the news or catching up on the latest events. He is a nerdy boy.

Jonathan Ball

Jonathan Ball needs to be impossible.

Ball successfully creates a book that has not and can never exist in the realm of literature.

His best feature is his flaw.

Souvankham Thammavongsa

Ironically, she was born in the same year that her mother gave birth. She was not an active participant in her birth, that was mostly done by her parents.

Thammavongsa's metaphysical thermometer becomes a symbol of a thermometer by her description of "a thermometer."

AMERICAN LITERATURE
Edgar Allan Poe

In "The Cask," the narrator, Montressor, used flashbacks to aid in portraying himself as unreliable.

If Montressor had died during the murder, he would not have been able to find the time to write this story. It would not have been the right mindset.

The narrator has a way of telling a story 50 years later that, frankly, I just don't believe anymore.

The trowel casts a foreshadow.

He tells the story so well he doesn't even need to be reliable.

Walt Whitman

Poor Walt Whitman, wrote rich and lived broke.

Emily Dickinson

Emily Dickinson is so baised against her own death. That's how she gains my trust.

Sadly, Dickinson's writing invokes thought in her readers.

Poets are obliged to convey a thousand messages with their form, and much more than prose. In a single dash of space we can see the polished and analysed core of words. For example, the death by horse beat.

The poet's pause signalifies death.

Frank Baum and *The Wizard of Oz*

There are similarities between the film and the novel on which it is based.

Some films that are based on books are successful, but in that case, it is always the opposite.

Baum did not want to have morals.

Even Glenda's equivalent, the Witch of the North has a pointed cap used to summon a chalkboard.

Henry James and *The Turn of the Screw*

The Turn of the Screw is about how when people feel guilty about having sex with children they turn into ghosts and take it out on others. The bottom line is you shouldn't tell children your sex.

Henry James would rather not know what his readers think.

The groups sit around the fire exchanging ghosts. In *The Turn of the Screw*, the reader is introduced to the narrator knows who.

The credibility of the narrator is diminished due to the author's lack of knowledge and instability.

The fact that the author had a brother who was a psychotic makes even this book seem crazy. It is hard to do anything to deny it.

James' work captures the genre of a gothic which turns out to be a ghost.

He hangs the reader and leaves them there.

Ursula K. Le Guin

This story is a metaphor for third word countries.

It is awfully unkind to torture a child. The society probably lacks kindness, too.

Tillie Olsen

Emily had to man up. In this case, though, she had to woman up.

The word "shoogily" is full of euphonic sounds that reminds me of my mother.

DEFINITIONS II

Solecism

Solar rhyming.

The beginning of sound.

Breaking the rules of rhythm.

Breaking no grammar.

The breaking of nothing.

Only the speaker in a poem, the soul speaker.

Sometimes a kys is just a kiss.

Violated words.

The fear of being alone.

The space between letters.

Soulasian: breaking in grammar.

Solecism: when a words has something to do with sound poetry.

Alliteration

Alliteration: how articulation people pronounce words.

Alliteration is when two words touch.

Putting words back together again.

The ability to read every word in a text.

Alliteration: a series of words beginning with the same word.

Anagram

Anagram: the funny of language.

Anagram: Taking the letters from one word and giving them to another.

A puzzle, like a newspaper.

The definition of an anagram is a pallindrome.

Like baking with language.

Lines that create a word/phrase/category when read vertically or horizontally.

Taking the letters of dear and having them read.

Anagram: talking to letters about themselves.

Words that share an alphabet.

Consonance

Consonance: the flow. As in, don't stop the flow.

A constant sound.

Consonance: when words make sounds.

Consonance: sounds familiar.

Constant change in wordplay.

Disjunctive

Disjunctive: when words no longer mean.

Words that don't like each other.

Breakwriting.

Homonym

Homonym: same word, different channel.

Hominem: against something. Against meaning.

The opposite of word.

Genre

Genre is the mood and language of a text.

Genre is vagueness and overlap; either intentionally or by the reader. It is arguably the author's responsibility.

Genres are categories or fields by which people buy books.

The genre of a book is not real.

A Satire is a piece of literature not to be taken seriously.

Realism brings out the ugly truth of ugly people.

Genre is shown to be a discussion of women's identity and sexuality.

PROFOUND FORISMS II

Since the early days, sound has played a central role in music.

Death is evident in this text as everyone dies.

Murder is the act of killing another without their permission.

It is important to clarify that a novel is not a bad thing.

His isolation leaves him solitary.

The use of language is important in writing poetry. Without the use of language, a poem is not the same.

Language is only limited by humans.

W is an exhausting sound.

Culture is not uncivil. Farming is not savage.

Civilization is the feminized male.

Sometimes a word is as simple as sounds.

As the professor said, the truth cannot be frowned.

To be a stereotype one must conquer thinking.

Doubt sequences come from dreams.

Racism was invented in the past to spite the future. Language is all the evidence we need.

If the book was written in a different way, the reader would have a different experience.

Change is a one way street to representing difference.

For whom is the daylight? And for how long?

Visually the audience sees.

Free will is defined as the ability to act at one's own desertion.

Language can fruit identity.

The reader is an emotion found in the text.

ONE-OFFS

One serious problem

It is a problem that has existed in society since time.

Lucky Guy

It's tit for tod.

Invisibility is a problem with ghosts

Her view about the ghosts was biased because she stereotyped them and did not see her bias.

The ghosts believe in themselves in ways we cannot see.

Some even I can't make sense of...

Leonard Cohen's poetry is poultry which helps the reader to relate and perhaps connect to their own life experience.

Perhaps a bit too general?

Essentially the story discusses people in society and how they are viewed by others.

Combines the Heroin & Artist-Ego Story

Nick Craine injects his own voice.

MISSPELLED AUTHOR NAMES

One student found her dry

Margaret Allwood

The experimental poet whose poetry follows tightly conceived rules

Christian Box   (Christian Bök)

The contentious psychologist

Sigmund Feud

A clean and effeminate philosopher

Neatshe

But he's made a place for himself

Niche

The famous writer of the little details in life

Alice Minnow

I Love Moosey?

Mucy Maude Montgomery

Happy Brides?

Marry Shelley

Merry Shelley

Alexandra Popes makes a mockery of her
hummer.

Franstein

She really wasn't happy

Susanas Moody

The Light of Canadian Confederation Poetry

Archibald Lampon

Other Misspelled Author Names

Barbra Growdy

Samuel the Chaplain

Helen Sioux

Great Essay Titles

"Obasan's Junk"

"George Elliott Clarke's *Whylah Falls*: Carving Out an Identity with Water"

"Canadian Identity After Leonard Cohen Got a Convertible"

"Presummtions are Generalizations"

Misspelled Titles

As Form Me and My House

As For Me in My House

Some of My Beloved

As the Mits Leave no Scar

The Problems of Being Ernie

And of mine own self, untrue

Professor Beattes

Professor Grag Betts

Proof Betts

Grey Betts

"G"

Punctuation is another quagmire of possible errors

Henry James's's

Even the use of quotation marks can be confusing or amusing

"Professor" Betts

DEFINITIONS III

The Connotation of Denotation

The denotation of the word "weird" is something that is not normal. The connotation of "weird" is funky.

The word "library" connotates someplace where young people like to hang out. The denotation of "library" means stress, anxiety, homework, and an overwhelming amount of knowledge.

The word I have chosen is long. When seeing this word connotations of length arise.

Staircase: denotatively they are essentially elevated ground levels that help us get down stairs.

The Crisis and Poetic Form

Crisis: a large problem known as literature.

Poetic form: when words have feelings.

Crisis is an issue on the brink of coming to a head

The plot is the place where the story occurs to itself.

The conflict is the opposite side of the character.

Crisis is one simple huge moment of enormous problematic happening in a book.

Poetic form: when a stanza grows up to become a poem.

Crisis is the tense moment of language in a text.

Poetic form is how you tell a poem from nothing.

A crisis is a story compared to a conflict in a narrative with a climax.

Conflict: when an author fights his characters.

Figurative Language

To speak in metaphors, figurative language
is a way of saying that you don't know what
something truly is.

The antagonist is the one who calls the police.

The Antagonist can also be the US.

Plot is the sequins of event. It revolves around a
central pole.

Story is the events that happened last night. Plot
is how I got away with it.

Our heads weren't blown, but our figurative
language sure was.

Figurative language is language that differs from a
figurative sense of this word.

It is the meaning of language when it cannot be
said.

Figurative language is what you use when you don't want to be taken seriously.

Figurative language aren't literally words.

It is the evolution of language.

Types of Humour

An improbable intervention that resolves the complications of the plot is called a pun.

Satire is only in Ireland.

Parody: an imitation of funny.

Pun: when the meaning of a word is impaired.

Irony: saying something funny that's totally not.

Satire: when a character uses a funny voice.

Satire: making fun of someone without telling them.

Parody: a political campaign in the US where the candidates are donkies and elephants.

Satire: ridicules humans for failing.

Pun: a one-liner worth catching.

Imitation: an attempt to become a genre that you aren't.

Parody: to mimic something like *Saturday Night Live*.

Irony: portraying something that actually means something.

Malapropism: weird words.

Irony: using something to mean something in a serious way.

Satire: the opposite of your desire.

Pun: play on words (ie leave the tree alone).

Satire is enjoyable because it does not make you think.

Irony: saying something and meaning it not.

Using your own creativity is an example of forcing sillyness on humour.

Satire: A piece of literature consisting only of Ireland during their food shortage.

Hyperbole: an exaggeration run a mock.

Gregory Betts is an award-winning author, editor and professor at Brock University in St. Catharines, Ontario. He has been teaching literature for a dozen years now at four different universities in Canada and Germany. He has published five books of poetry, edited five books of experimental Canadian writing, and recently published *Avant-Garde Canadian Literature: The Early Manifestations* (University of Toronto Press, 2012). He is currently the Director of the Centre for Canadian Studies and Graduate Program Director of Canadian and American Studies at Brock University in St. Catharines, Ontario.